U.S. Diplomatic
1750–1945

Walter LaFeber

Historical Association

WALTER LaFEBER is Noll Professor of History at Cornell University. His most recent book is *The American Age: The United States at Home and Abroad since 1750* (Norton, 1989).

This essay originally appeared in *The New American History*, published by Temple University Press in the series Critical Perspectives on the Past, edited by Susan Porter Benson, Stephen Brier, and Roy Rosenzweig. Copyright © 1990 Temple University.

This edition published by the American Historical Association
ISBN: 0-87229-063-8
Printed in the United States of America

▶ **The New American History**

SERIES
EDITED
BY
ERIC FONER

Liberty and Power:
History,

by

American

► Contents

▶ **Essays in** *The New American History* **series**

► Introduction

IN THE COURSE OF THE PAST TWENTY YEARS, AMERICAN HISTORY HAS BEEN remade. Inspired initially by the social movements of the 1960s and 1970s—which shattered the "consensus" vision that had dominated historical writing—and influenced by new methods borrowed from other disciplines, American historians redefined the very nature of historical study. The rise of the "new histories," the emphasis on the experience of ordinary Americans, the impact of quantification and cultural analysis, the eclipse of conventional political and intellectual history—these trends are now so widely known (and the subject of such controversy) that they need little reiteration. The study of American history today looks far different than it did a generation ago.

This series comprises essays written by thirteen scholars—many of whom have been at the forefront of the transformation of historical study—each assessing recent developments in historians' understanding of a period or a major theme in the nation's past. The idea for the collection originated with a request from the American Historical Association for a series of pamphlets addressed specifically to high school teachers of American history and designed to familiarize them with the most up-to-date historical scholarship.

ERIC FONER

After a false start or two the proposal, somewhat revised, was adopted and published as a collection by Temple University Press, and now, separately, by the AHA. *The New American History* is addressed to a wide audience: students, teachers, and the broad public concerned with the current state of American historical study.

Each author was given a free hand in developing his or her reflections. No attempt has been made to fit the essays into a predetermined mold or impose a single point of view or interpretive framework. Nonetheless, certain themes recur with remarkable regularity, demonstrating how pervasively the "new histories" have reshaped our understanding of the American past.

If anything is characteristic of the recent study of American history, it is attention to the experience of previously neglected groups—not simply as an addition to a preexisting body of knowledge but as a fundamental redefinition of history itself. Women's history has greatly expanded its subject area, moving beyond the movement for suffrage, which preoccupied earlier women historians, into such previously ignored realms as the history of sexuality. Labor history, from a field that defined its subject as the experience of wage workers in factories and the activities of unionized workers, has expanded to encompass the study of slaves, women at home, and the majority of laborers, who in America have always been unorganized.

Even more striking, perhaps, is that African-American history and women's history have matured to the point where they are not widely recognized as legitimate subfields with their own paradigms and debates but are seen as indispensable to any understanding of the broad American experience. These points are made effectively in surveys of the two fields by Thomas Holt and Linda Gordon, but they are evident in other contributions as well. Richard McCormick makes clear that any calculus of Americans' gains and losses in the late nineteenth and early twentieth centuries must take into account the severe reverses suffered by blacks in those years. William Chafe places the civil rights movement at the center of his analysis of social change in post–World War II America. My own essay on the Civil War era argues not only that slavery and emancipation were the central issues in the sectional crisis but that blacks were active agents in shaping the era's history.

Women's history, too, has forced historians not simply to compensate for their previous neglect of one-half of the population but to rethink some of their basic premises. Linda Kerber delineates how the

American Revolution affected prevailing definitions of "manhood" and "womanhood" and how patriarchy itself was restructured as a result of the revolutionary crisis. Leon Fink emphasizes the obvious but long-ignored fact that women have always been part of the country's labor history. Sean Wilentz shows that a key result of economic changes in the Jacksonian era was an ideological division between the public sphere of men and the private sphere of women.

Many of the essays also demonstrate the impact of new methods on recent historical study. John Murrin shows how historical demography has yielded a new estimate of the human toll exacted by the colonization of the New World and how epidemiology affects our understanding of the decimation of the hemisphere's original inhabitants. Alice Kessler-Harris outlines the ways in which the "new empiricism" of statistical analysis has helped shape developments in social history. Richard McCormick and Alan Brinkley assess the impact of modernization theory on the study of both pre– and post–World War I periods.

Despite the apparent ascendancy of social history, these essays do not lend credence to recent complaints that historians are no longer concerned with politics, economics, the Constitution, and intellectual history. Such traditional concerns appear in virtually every essay, although often in forms that earlier historians might find unrecognizable. The old "presidential synthesis"—which understood the evolution of American society chiefly via presidential elections and administrations—is dead (and not lamented). And "politics" now means much more than the activities of party leaders. Some essays devote attention to the broad political culture or "public life" of a particular era; others stress the role of the state itself in American history and the ways various groups have tried to use it for their own purposes.

Alan Brinkley, for example, discusses the New Deal within the context of the constraints imposed on government by the nature of America's political and economic institutions, and the general impact of the period on the evolution of the American state. And Walter LaFeber shows how the Constitution has helped to shape the evolution of American foreign policy.

Many historians have lamented of late the failure of the current generation of scholars to produce a modern "synthesis" of the American past. Older synthetic interpretations, ranging from Frederick Jackson Turner's frontier thesis to the consensus view of the 1950s, have been shattered, but no new one has emerged to fill the void. Indeed, the very diversity of the "new histories" and the portrait of America they have created seem to have fragmented historical scholarship and impeded the attempt to create a coherent new vision of the national experience. Several of the essays echo this concern, but there is sufficient similarity in their approaches and interpretations to suggest that the fragmentation of historical study may have been overstated. If the essays do not, and by their very nature cannot, produce the widely called-for new synthesis, several do point in that direction. Sean Wilentz, for example, suggests that the social, political, and economic history of Jacksonian America can be integrated into a coherent whole by placing the market revolution at the center of the account. McCormick demonstrates that a "public life" can be a flexible, imaginative concept, capable of integrating a variety of social, economic, and political developments.

As this series demonstrates, American history is a field of remarkable diversity and vitality. Its practitioners continue to grapple with the most pressing issues and persistent themes of our national experience: definitions of liberty and equality, causes of social change, the exercise of political power. Today, popular knowledge—or lack of knowledge—of the nation's past has once again become a subject of intense public discussion. Certainly, the more all of us—students, teachers, and other citizens—know of our national experience, the better. But as these essays illustrate, American history at its best remains not simply a collection of facts, not a politically sanctioned listing of indisputable "truths," but an ongoing mode of collective self-discovery about the nature of our society.

ERIC FONER
Columbia University

▶ ▶ ▶ ▶ ▶ ▶ ▶ ▶ ▶ ▶ ▶ ▶ ▶ ▶

LIBERTY AND POWER: U.S. DIPLOMATIC HISTORY, 1750–1945

Walter LaFeber

AMERICAN DIPLOMATIC HISTORY BECAME A POPULAR CLASSROOM SUBJECT IN THE 1930s and 1940s. In those decades Americans began to realize that their overseas expansion after 1898 had made the nation a leading military power and the globe's greatest economic force. They were also discovering that events thousands of miles away directly shaped their own lives: a failed European banking system in 1931 forced people out of work in the American Midwest; Japanese aggression in China during 1940 led to the conscription of American men while the United States was officially at peace.

In 1783 George Washington proclaimed this new country "our rising empire." By the close of World War II it had fully risen. The United States was the globe's superpower militarily, economically, and culturally. When, after 1945, a U.S. president secretly decided to change a government in Italy, Iran, Vietnam, Lebanon, or the Belgian Congo, he possessed the power to enforce his decision and shape the lives of people in distant—and, to most Americans, unknown—nations. Such power raised central issues: what were the values and traditions that shaped and guided it? Could such power actually be used to benefit different peoples? Were Americans capable of becoming global policemen without endangering their own

1

prosperity and constitutional liberties? The nation's diplomatic history had to be understood before such pivotal questions could be answered.

Diplomatic historians discovered that they were uniquely qualified to deal with such fundamental issues. They were uniquely qualified, that is, if they understood that diplomatic history is not simply a story of "what one clerk told another" (as a scholar once described it). American foreign relations are made up of the politics, cultures, and economic relationships that determine what a U.S. clerk tells a foreign counterpart. Properly crafted, diplomatic history analyzes the relationships not only between nations but between peoples within those nations that shape their foreign policies. It moves across both national boundaries and scholarly disciplines, using such a diverse and wide-reaching approach to attain a central goal: to discover and explain the *power* that determines those inter- and intranational relationships in a world increasingly interdependent. Thus the teaching of U.S. foreign policy can become the framework within which many other crucial events of American history must be understood. And such teaching can identify the points at which the everyday concerns of Americans interact with those of the global community in which they live.

The nature of that larger community, however, has constantly changed. The "world" that preoccupied Americans in the early nineteenth century was Spanish Florida, or British-Indian alliances in the Mississippi Valley. The world that preoccupies Americans in the late twentieth century stretches around the globe and into the heavens. The values, even the political system, that Americans employ in dealing with those different worlds have nevertheless remained remarkably constant. U.S. diplomatic history, therefore, should explain the nature of power in the international system, analyze America's reciprocal relationships within the international arena, and, in understanding this complex past, reveal the steps we took as a people to reach the position we occupy in our own time. It should also reveal how the past has determined the purposes we now have for using a power undreamed of even by Washington when he prophesied a rising American empire.

INTERPRETIVE OVERVIEWS

The most important general interpretations of U.S. diplomatic history have shared two characteristic approaches. The first has been to explain past foreign policy in order to provide insight into contemporary problems. The second has been to relate internal and external policies—so closely that the line between domestic and foreign affairs has frequently blurred.

The "realist" school of the 1950s aimed at reshaping Americans' views of their world by revising their views of the past. The realists argued that to survive in the modern world, Americans had to understand the realities of power (especially military power) and understand as well that the United States was not all that different from other nations. It was just one more player in a global diplomatic game whose rules were balance-of-power politics. The American system thus acted on the world stage much like other powers, such as eighteenth-century France or nineteenth-century England. Realist scholars emphasized that the Founders of 1776 and 1787 had scored their historic successes because they understood and acted upon these principles in carrying out early American foreign policy. But unfortunately, the realist historians continued, by the late nineteenth century the Founders' tough-minded world view had been replaced by "legalism and moralism." These new traits led U.S. officials to place their faith in such abstract ideals as international law and enlightened public opinion, rather than power politics, to preserve peace and American prosperity. These "idealists," the realists contended, mistakenly viewed the United States as unique and believed that this very uniqueness (such as the supposed good effects of democratic public opinion) could replace military force as the determinant of global affairs.

George F. Kennan's *American Diplomacy, 1900 to 1950* (1951) remains the best-known statement of the realist position. In Kennan's view, U.S. policy during the formative years between 1898 and 1920, when the United States became a world power, was too often shaped by misplaced faith in legalisms and morality, or overly influenced by other nations who manipulated somewhat naive Washington officials. Kennan argued, for example, that the United States became an important power in Asia during 1898–1900 not because Americans understood their real interests in Asian affairs but because they were maneuvered by British officials to support an "open door" policy, defined by U.S. Secretary of State John Hay as a "fair field and no favor" for all nations competing in the China market. This policy, Kennan and other realists believed, benefited the interests of Great Britain, not the United States. Kennan went on to argue that Woodrow Wilson was so taken with abstract legal and moral concerns (such as "making the world safe for democracy") that as president he never understood the realities of world power. Consequently, he helped the Allies destroy Germany between 1917 and 1920 and thereby also destroyed any hope of a healthy, long-term European balance of power; such a balance required a stable Germany at its center. Perhaps, Kennan suggested, Wilson's policies made Americans feel more righteous in the aftermath of World War I, but they created a power vacuum in central Europe that was soon filled by Nazi militarism and Soviet expansionism.

The realist approach has been refined and elaborated in a series of influential books by Norman Graebner. His studies span the length of U.S. diplomatic history, but he has focused on certain turningpoints: the 1840s

4

expansionism into Mexico and to the Pacific, the Civil War, and the Cold War years. Graebner emphasizes what he calls the "means-ends" question: whether the United States had the means at a specific point to achieve its diplomatic ends. Too often, he concludes, Americans were guided not by a realistic understanding of the power they held but by unrealistic beliefs in the power of morality and legality. Such beliefs led officials such as Wilson to reach for foreign policy objectives that were unobtainable. Graebner worries especially about the tendency of Americans, when they become disillusioned by the failure of their morality to create a better world, to resort to dangerous military means. Thus, when President Wilson failed to make Mexico and the Caribbean nations democratic by preaching to them, he sent in the Marines. And thus, Graebner argues, when Americans forgot about the limits of their power and were guided instead by a simplistic and confused anti-Communism, they became immersed in Vietnam.

The realists concentrated their attention on elite officials, those few at the top level who made and carried out foreign policy. They showed less interest in the complex social and economic levels of American society that produced those officials and their ideologies. By the 1960s the realist approach was being challenged by scholars who were interested in examining the entire society, not just the elite. Going beyond the political and intellectual history employed by the realists, the new scholars also stressed the importance of the links between economic change and foreign policy. In the work of the "revisionists," as these younger scholars came to be known, the distinction between domestic and foreign affairs virtually disappeared.

Of special importance in the revisionist school were three books by William Appleman Williams. *The Tragedy of American Diplomacy* (1959) is a short book with a large thesis: since at least the 1890s the open-door approach shaped not only U.S. policy in China (as Kennan and most historians believed) but American diplomacy worldwide. Moreover, Williams directly contradicted Kennan by demonstrating that the open-door policy was engineered not by British officials but by U.S. leaders who fully understood, and were determined to expand, their nation's economic interests. Williams stressed the economic component, but he also reinterpreted that component as the ideology for twentieth-century American policy in general. As Bradford Perkins observed in 1984, much of the work published in diplomatic history after 1960 has been a dialogue with Williams's book.

Williams expanded his argument in *The Contours of American History* (1961), in which he blended domestic and foreign affairs into one coherent interpretation of the entire American experience. In exploring the sources of power in an evolving American society, he divided the nation's history into three phases: the age of "mercantilism," from colonial times until the 1820s, when the state's power guided private enterprise; the age of "laissez-nous faire," from the 1820s to the 1890s, when power fragmented and the legend of American individualism appeared amid rampant continental expansionism; and the age of the corporation after the 1890s. In 1969 Williams published *The Roots of the Modern American Empire*, which asserted that agrarian interests, threatened by suffocating crop surpluses after the Civil War, framed the argument about how to dispose of this glut of goods and reached a solution that anticipated the twentieth-century policies of an industrialized America. That solution, Williams argued, was to conquer world markets and employ, if necessary, direct government help to do so. He concluded that this policy transformed John Winthrop's seventeenth-century Christian vision of a virtuous American "City on a Hill," radiating its power by its own example, into a worldwide empire extending its power by military and economic force. Williams's emphasis on the integral relationship between domestic and foreign policies influenced other historians, including many who disagreed with his emphasis on the economic sources of U.S. diplomacy.

The revisionists' concern with the domestic sources of diplomacy served as the starting point for a more recent attempt to provide a general framework for understanding the nation's foreign policy. Thomas J. McCormick believes that the concept of "corporatism" can reveal the forces that drove that policy. Within this concept the University of Wisconsin scholar includes the country's large functional groups—government, business, labor organizations—working in voluntary but close association. These groups, McCormick argues, have cooperated at a private rather than a governmental level to shape national policies; hence, their activities have often been missed by the media. Fundamental to the corporatists' power, he adds, has been their belief in and control over "productionism"—that is, maximum production that enlarges the economic pie for everyone. To the corporatists, emphasizing maximum production has been preferable to creating political mechanisms for redistributing wealth. The ultimate political mechanism for redistributing wealth, after all, is revolution.

Historians have used variations of corporatism to understand two pivotal eras: the Progressive years of 1913 to 1933, and the early Cold War years of 1945 to 1953. Woodrow Wilson and Herbert Hoover, the argument runs, were the key figures in the attempt to create a cooperative arrangement between government, labor, and business groups. The aim of corporatism was not only to ameliorate problems in the United States but, by helping others produce ever greater amounts of wealth, to raise living standards and thus abort revolutionary movements in Latin America and central and eastern Europe. Revolutionary class warfare could be replaced with class cooperation. Wilson outlined such economic and political cooperation in his Fourteen Points speech of 1918. The address asked all powers to comply voluntarily with those diplomatic principles (the open-door policy, "freedom of the seas," self-determination) which he believed could most effectively increase production and trade, as well as distribute the resulting wealth in an orderly, nonrevolutionary manner.

The significance of Wilson as a seminal figure in modern American foreign policy and the importance of understanding the antirevolutionary theme in that policy, was stressed by Arno Mayer in two influential works, *Political Origins of the New Diplomacy, 1917–1918* (1959) and *Politics and Diplomacy at Peacemaking: Containment and Counterrevolution at Versailles, 1918–1919* (1967). Emphasizing the close relationship of domestic politics and foreign policy, Mayer showed that severe internal problems had created fears in Europe and the United States that Bolshevism would triumph in the West. That fear in turn led Wilson and Europe's leaders to focus on containing Bolshevism rather than on building a healthy Europe. In more recent scholarship, Lloyd Gardner has agreed with Mayer that the Wilson presidency marks the place to begin understanding many of the problems that have plagued twentieth-century U.S. foreign policy. But the Rutgers University historian has taken the argument a step further. He believes (contrary to Kennan and other realists) that Wilson fully understood that United States interests required an orderly and open world system. The president assumed that his nation's liberal principles could best produce such a system, but when he attempted to apply them in such countries as Mexico, Russia, and Haiti, they seemed to produce more, not less, revolution. Wilson then resorted to military power to realize his dream of an orderly system. In *Covenant with Power* (1984), Gardner argues not only that Wilson's policy led him into repeated military interventions but that his successors—from Calvin Coolidge to Ronald Reagan—also found that a commitment to opposing revolutions and promoting democracy continually led them to use military force.

Robert Wiebe characterized the Progressive era as *The Search for Order* (1967). Foreign policy leaders headed that search both through their efforts for cooperation (corporatism) at home and their beliefs that productionism and antirevolutionary policies were prerequisites for order abroad. Michael Hogan's *Informal Entente* (1977) demonstrates how a variant of corporatism characterized American foreign policy–making during the 1920s. In *The Marshall Plan* (1987), Hogan uses the corporatist approach to analyze fundamentals of the massive and historic effort to rebuild western Europe after World War II. That book is one of several published in the 1980s that takes corporatism to a quite different level. Whereas the term had been used to show the links between U.S. internal decision-making and the nation's foreign affairs, it has come to mean an approach that can open insights into policy-making in the entire Western capitalist world. Capitalism is viewed less as a national phenomenon than as a world system. Foreign policies follow the requirements of that system. Thus, American diplomatic history has become the discipline that can explain how pre-1945 U.S. foreign policy, shaped largely by domestic needs, was transformed into a foreign policy increasingly influenced by an international marketplace and a culture created by a new technology and late twentieth-century capitalism that have little respect for national borders. Thomas McCormick's *American Half-Century* (1990) is a key analysis of how that transformation occurred.

Having started with accounts of "what one clerk told another," American diplomatic history has moved on to demonstrate how a complex domestic system shapes foreign policy and, more recently, how an increasingly integrated world system (or what has been called "the global village") determines Americans' interactions with that system. No other field is better equipped to trace these fundamental changes, because only diplomatic history is able to trace the links between domestic and foreign affairs and, at the same time, properly place those relationships within the context of the constantly shifting power relationships in the international system. From this perspective, American history is largely, and increasingly, international history.

CHRONOLOGICAL OVERVIEW

If the "revisionist" historians have shaped the debate over post-1890 U.S. foreign policy, the "realists" continue to influence our view of the first generation of American diplomacy. But even studies of the Founders necessarily stress the importance of the larger international arena. As exemplified by James Hutson's *John Adams and the Diplomacy of the American Revolution* (1980), the realists have argued that throughout the 1776–1800 period, U.S. officials intelligently and profitably followed the principles of European power politics. Hutson demonstrates, for example, that the nation's commercial policy—its lifeline—was not based on any idealistic hope that foreign powers would unselfishly accept the American ideal of free trade. Instead, the policy rested on the principle of reciprocity: unless European nations welcomed U.S. exports of cotton and tobacco, Americans would not allow European goods into the United States. The Founders thus depended not on enlightened public opinion or morality but on economic self-interest and power politics.

Hutson applied this insight to the seminal document of U.S. foreign economic policy, John Adams's "model treaty" of 1776. Adams argued that the United States should use its economic power to enforce the treatment it wanted from other nations. If that economic weapon could be successfully employed, he continued, Americans would not have to protect themselves by entering dangerous political alliances with powerful European states. In Adams's hand, therefore, U.S. commerce became a weapon with two barrels: one would ensure that Americans had access to indispensable overseas markets, and the other would help guarantee that they could avoid entangling political alliances with more powerful nations. The United States would instead enjoy maximum freedom of action in world affairs (or what has become known in American history as "isolationism"). Adams's approach realistically utilized the nation's great strength, its commerce, to hide its political and military weaknesses.

Adams's generation, however, made one near-fatal mistake. It assumed that the loose confederation of American states could effectively regulate its commerce and also retaliate against Europeans who refused to treat Americans equitably. By 1786 the Europeans, led by the vengeful British, had declared economic warfare against the United States. Unable to exploit foreign markets, Americans sank into economic depression. That crisis in turn triggered internal riots, especially in western Massachusetts, and also threats from settlements beyond the Appalachians to leave the floundering United States and join the adjacent British and Spanish empires. In *Independence on Trial: Foreign Affairs and the Making of the Constitution* (1973, 1986), Frederick Marks III argues that these internal crises led directly to the calling of the Constitutional Convention in 1787. The delegates were determined to create a centralized government that could effectively regulate overseas commerce, conduct a vigorous foreign policy, and thus stabilize conditions at home. Domestic tranquillity depended so greatly on the capacity to carry out a successful foreign policy that the Founders had to design a new system possessing such a capability. In a world of cutthroat imperial rivalries, the United States had to develop its own more centralized imperial system in order to survive.

Once that system began operating in 1789, Americans fought bitterly over the question of which groups would control it. Again, the intimate relationship between domestic and foreign affairs appeared, for out of that fight arose the first American political party system. One faction organized around Alexander Hamilton's plan for centralizing power by, among other means, having the new government fund state debts. To pay off those debts, however, the central government needed revenue, especially from import taxes. Most U.S. imports came from Great Britain. Therefore, Hamilton urged a policy of friendship toward the British. That is, domestic needs dictated his foreign policy. But James Madison and Thomas Jefferson disagreed. They were more concerned with exports (especially from southern states) than imports. Consequently, they feared Great Britain, which heavily discriminated against U.S. goods, and preferred France, with whom the United States enjoyed a favorable balance of trade. The division between Hamiltonians and Jeffersonians was not simply along pro-British and pro-French lines but between factions that had different domestic interests. By 1796 the factions had begun to coalesce into Federalists and Democratic-Republicans. The first American party system was born.

A turningpoint in the history of the "rising empire" occurred with the War of 1812. In the 1960s historians viewed that conflict as an almost farcical war into which a weak President Madison was forced by fire-eating War Hawks from the West and South. J. C. A. Stagg's *Mr. Madison's War* (1983), however, has persuasively argued that it was the president, not Congress, who fully understood the vital U.S. interests at stake in 1810– 12 and that Madison shrewdly led the nation into war to protect those interests. He believed that Americans required a large overseas commerce to survive and that they should be free to sell in any markets they wished. The British refused to recognize that right; to defeat Napoleon, London officials tried to cut off U.S.-European trade by seizing American ships and sailors. Madison concluded that a threat of war and, if necessary, a U.S. invasion of Canada (long viewed as a "hostage" that Americans could use to pry concessions out of London) would so endanger British colonies in the New World that Great Britain would be forced to recognize American rights. The War of 1812 thus became another struggle for basic U.S. commercial liberties.

Madison had badly miscalculated, however. By using new findings in social and political history, Stagg demonstrates that Americans' first allegiance was not to the national government but to local interests. Throughout much of New England those parochial interests influenced merchants to work with the British fleet that controlled the seas. New England therefore refused to support the war and in 1814 even threatened to leave the Union. The president was finally saved by the end of the Napoleonic wars in Europe and major U.S. naval victories on the Great Lakes, victories that discouraged the British from continuing the fighting. With the European conflict ended, London was able to recognize greater U.S. rights on the high seas. The New England secessionist movement collapsed, and the section's merchants turned from their traditional British connections to other markets (as in newly independent Latin America) or to investing at home in the rising manufacturing complex. Stagg's work spells out on several levels the intimate relationship between domestic and foreign affairs at a pivotal point in the nation's history.

After 1815, Americans turned inward to settle the vast lands they had acquired in the 1783 peace treaty that ended the Revolution and in Jefferson's purchase of Louisiana in 1803. A key figure of the 1814 to 1844 years was Andrew Jackson—war hero, Anglophobe, Indian fighter, and two-term president. Robert Remini's three-volume biography (1977–84) argues that Jackson's military exploits were primarily responsible for the U.S. ability to annex Florida between 1818 and 1821 and also for the 1819

Transcontinental Treaty with Spain that provided the first U.S. claim to the Pacific coast. Remini's interpretations have been questioned from several directions, however. One criticism draws from older work showing that the shrewd diplomacy of Secretary of State John Quincy Adams was more important to these U.S. successes than Jackson's activities. Adams's handling of Spanish, British, and Russian threats in Florida and along the northwest coast, as well as his pivotal role in formulating the Monroe Doctrine's principles in 1823, have led scholars to rank him as the greatest secretary of state in the nation's history.

A second criticism of Remini's approach has come from scholars exploiting findings in literary criticism, social history, and even psychiatry. Michael Rogin's *Fathers and Children: Andrew Jackson and the Subjugation of the American Indians* (1975) uses insights from psychiatry to explain Jackson's brutal treatment of British agents in Florida and Native Americans in Florida and elsewhere. Richard Drinnon's *Facing West* (1980) places the violent white expansionism of the nineteenth century within a four-hundred-year context of warfare against races Americans considered inferior. In this newer literature, Jackson becomes only a more interesting and famous example in a long line of leading Americans who resolved personal and social problems by subjugating others. In the hands of these scholars the frontier has become less the birthplace of democracy and economic equality (as it was characterized, for instance, in Frederick Jackson Turner's classic work) than a killing ground where European settlers and Native Americans savaged each other until the brutality infused white American consciousness. U.S. expansion no longer remained a tale of encounters between foreign ministers.

The expansionism climaxed during the 1840s. As their critics claimed, Americans were "amphibious animals" who moved aggressively on both land and sea. On land, the James K. Polk administration (1845–49) seized nearly half of Mexico, acquired the Oregon territory, and annexed the nine-year-old state of Texas, which had rebelled against Mexico. U.S. landholdings suddenly increased 50 percent. Overseas, the Whig leadership of Daniel Webster and other mercantile northeasterners worked out the first formal treaties with China in 1844 and with Japan a decade later. In the late 1840s U.S. officials began linking their continental conquests and Asian interests by staking out claims in Central America, where during the 1850s Americans built the first ocean-to-ocean railway.

This combination of mainland and transoceanic expansion has been labeled "American continentalism" by historian Charles Vevier, who provocatively insists that the two types of expansion have been closely related. Vevier demonstrates, for example, that the first ideas about building a transcontinental railroad in the United States came from men in the 1840s who understood the reciprocal relationship between expansion on land

and by sea. Building such a rail system, they reasoned, would not only link eastern producers with Pacific coast ports but develop the nation's interior and thus increase the amount of goods that could be sold in Asian markets. The development of the American continent would lead to the development of American interests in Asia—and vice versa.

David Pletcher's *Diplomacy of Annexation* (1973), the standard work on the 1840s, argues that the war against Mexico was unnecessary. A booming American population was searching for new lands to settle, Pletcher argues, and by waiting for that expanding population to sweep over California and the Southwest, Americans could have obtained peacefully what Polk acquired by sacrificing thousands of lives. Pletcher's view has been questioned in *James K. Polk: Continentalist, 1843–1846* (1966) by Charles Sellers, Polk's biographer, who uses fresh scholarship in political history to argue that Polk had little choice but to wage war. Powerful economic and social factions, found especially in the president's Democratic party, created a wave of expansionism that Polk rode into the White House—and war. Pletcher and Sellers nevertheless agree in discounting the old belief that a small conspiracy led by Polk or by southern slave interests caused the Mexican War. Rather, larger internal dynamics generated the expansionism. The system, not one man or one group, shaped foreign policies in the climactic 1840s.

Historians have also concluded that the 1840s marked a turn in white–Native American relations. Reginald Horsman's *Race and Manifest Destiny* (1981) identifies a growing conviction among whites that they had wrongly believed non-Caucasians could be peacefully assimilated into "civilized" society. By the 1840s the whites had concluded that Indians and Mexicans had to be eliminated, rather than assimilated, if white settlement were to progress. Thomas Hietala's *Manifest Design* (1985) continues the story by demonstrating a vital relationship between expansionism in the 1840s and in the 1890s. Before the publication of Hietala's work, historians saw little continuity between the earlier decade (when land expansion was dominant) and the later years (when Americans moved across water to conquer bases in the Caribbean and the Pacific). Now it appears that the racial views and the policy of military conquest of the 1840s triggered a series of wars with the Indians that lasted for nearly a half-century. Those conflicts opened much of the trans-Mississippi region to white settlement, allowed the building of transcontinental railroads and other key transportation systems, and thus developed the coherent, continental base that enabled the United States to emerge as a world power in the War of 1898. Again, internal change helped explain overseas triumphs. The Indian wars of the 1870s and 1880s, moreover, were important in developing the U.S. military that seized Spain's colonies in the Pacific and the Caribbean in 1898. During the 1880s a leading British military officer declared that the

U.S. Army was, man for man, the best fighting force in the world. As Hietala demonstrates, the post-1840 Indian policies helped make it that way.

Other studies have found similar continuity between American expansion into Asia in the 1840s and the 1890s. A common characteristic was that both periods of expansion followed economic depression in the United States. (Indeed, it seems that each time a severe economic downturn has struck the United States, Americans have become intensely interested in the China market—as in the 1780s, 1840s, 1890s, 1930s, and 1970s–early 1980s.) In both the 1840s and 1890s the search for profits was accompanied by a U.S. policy that tried to block European attempts to colonize parts of Asia. That policy emerged in part out of American pride in winning the first modern anticolonial struggle in 1776. This pride was complemented by the realization that any parts of Asia colonized by Europeans could be closed to American business and missionaries. U.S. officials consequently insisted on an open-door principle in Asia as early as the 1840s and finally obtained reluctant consent to the principle from Europeans and Japanese in 1899–1900. In *The Making of a Special Relationship* (1983), a work that provides an overall analysis of U.S.-China encounters to 1914, Michael Hunt argues that Washington's concern to keep China whole and non-colonized produced that "special relationship" but the relationship was complex: Americans were interested not merely in protecting the Chinese but in exploiting their markets.

Hunt's use of Chinese sources reveals, moreover, that China's officials shrewdly manipulated the foreigners, playing off American against European in an attempt to control all the intruders. Wrongly assuming that the Chinese were showing them special favor, Americans developed a too innocent view of China's foreign policy. In reality, the Chinese had long looked down on Americans as "second-chop Englishmen" who deserved little better treatment than other imperialists. Thus the Chinese fear of and antipathy to U.S. power in the post-1949 era had roots deep in the nineteenth century.

The 1890s were a watershed decade in American foreign policy. As noted above, its key events were parts of long-term developments that had begun much earlier in the century, but the decade also witnessed changes that mark the beginnings of modern American foreign policy. In those years the United States forced the British to recognize that it was now the paramount power in the Western Hemisphere. It was also during those years that newly powerful industrial and banking groups played the major role in shaping U.S. foreign policy for the first time. Instead of being preoccupied with finding overseas markets for raw cotton and wheat, as they had been for a century, U.S. exporters searched for customers of cotton textiles, agricultural machinery, and even locomotives that American factories were producing overabundantly. The first important U.S. multinational corporations appeared in the 1880s and 1890s, led by such well-known firms as Singer Sewing Machine (which established profitable subsidiaries in Russia), Eastman Kodak, and Standard Oil. The dynamic of American expansion was transformed: after four hundred years of seeking landed frontiers, it was looking for buyers of industrial goods and bank capital. If land was acquired, it was to be used not for farming but for naval bases in Hawaii, the Caribbean, and the Philippines that could protect the growing overseas commerce.

Finally, the 1890s produced a more centralized governmental apparatus to run foreign policy efficiently. Between 1897 and 1901 that apparatus was controlled by President William McKinley. Recent scholarly work has viewed McKinley as the first modern chief executive because of his ability to dominate Congress and his willingness to use military force overseas without congressional sanction. The military dimension of late nineteenth-century expansionism has gained special attention. In an original but neglected work, *Gray Steel and Blue Water Navy* (1979), B. Franklin Cooling demonstrates that domestic economic interests and foreign policy needs combined to build the first ships of the modern U.S. Navy. Officials realized that they needed a great fleet to protect growing overseas interests and understood that the nation's powerful iron and steel complex could create such a force. Thus emerged the military-industrial alliance. The relationship was not always smooth; Washington officials were not pleased, for example, when Andrew Carnegie tried to sell them steel at higher prices than he was charging the Russians. But need dictated compromise, and by the War of 1898 the military-industrial alliance had produced the Great White Fleet that won the war and could project its power to the distant Pacific.

McKinley first utilized that power, but he did so with little public flair. Theodore Roosevelt, on the other hand, bragged that he used the White House as "a bully pulpit" to summon Americans to assume world power. The flamboyant New Yorker seldom tried to escape public attention, even if courting it meant making defiant demands on other (usually weaker) governments or going off to shoot wild animals in Africa. But since Howard K. Beale's pathbreaking *Theodore Roosevelt and the Rise of America to World Power* (1956), we have understood that the private diplomat was more cautious than the public president. After 1904, for example, he worried that the Japanese and Russians were violating open-door principles and shutting Americans out of large parts of China. But he also knew that the United States could never fight a successful war against other powers on the Asian mainland simply to uphold the open-door principle, so he tried instead to work out a settlement with the Japanese. In Latin America, where U.S. power did dominate, his use of force was less restrained. In his search for order and markets, he used naval power in 1904–5 to stop a revolution in Santo Domingo and protect U.S. shipping and banking interests. Those reasons for the intervention, which became known as the Roosevelt Corollary to the Monroe Doctrine, established important precedents for later chief executives who sent troops into the Caribbean region.

Roosevelt and Woodrow Wilson grew to hate each other, but the latter found he had to follow many of the former's policies, especially in Latin America, where Wilson used force on a half-dozen occasions to stop internal upheavals. The most important recent analyses of Wilson's foreign policies, however, have also focused on two other questions. The first is why the president decided, with great reluctance, to take the United States into the massive slaughter of World War I. In the 1950s historians believed that the German declaration in January 1917 of all-out submarine warfare forced Wilson into the conflict. That declaration now appears a necessary but not sufficient explanation for the American decision. Wilson's leading biographer, Arthur Link, has concluded that the determination to be a full participant at the postwar peace conference was of special importance in the decision. Link and others have shown that Wilson believed he could obtain agreement to principles critical to U.S. domestic interests (such as freedom of the seas and liberal international trade) only by becoming a full participant in the shaping of the postwar world. He thus entered the conflict not only to ensure the defeat of Germany but to produce a peace that would truly make the world "safe for democracy" and other American interests.

There is less agreement among historians about the second question, how and why Wilson dealt with the first major twentieth-century revolutions. His most important challenge was handling the danger of Lenin's Bolshevik policies at the 1919 Paris Peace Conference. As the young journalist and presidential adviser Walter Lippmann observed at the time, Lenin was not invited to Paris, but his shadow hovered over every discussion because war-devastated Europe was a powder keg waiting to explode into Communist revolution. Most scholars now believe that Wilson failed to create the kind of democratic Europe he wanted because he was trapped between conservative (even reactionary) western European leaders and the eastern revolutionaries. No one could have developed a workable compromise between those two forces. More specifically, historians see Wilson trapped between Bolshevism and his faith in self-determination. He came to recognize that self-determination might actually lead to Communist states. When Hungarians and Germans threatened to elect Communists in 1919, the president chose to contain the threatened spread of radicalism, even if it meant sacrificing his ideal of self-determination.

The Republican officials who made U.S. foreign policy in the 1920s never resolved this growing tension between the principle of self-determination and the threat of radical revolution. Scholars agree that Washington policy-makers during this decade were little interested in Wilson's view of self-determination; they were dedicated instead to using the immense U.S. financial resources (many of which resulted from loans made to the belligerents during the Great War) to rebuild the world along capitalist lines. As noted above, the key word applied by historians to these policies is "corporatism" (or "associationalism.") U.S. bankers and exporters, for example, worked together to capture overseas markets—a combination that might have been illegal at home because of antitrust laws. But U.S. officials encouraged such cooperation overseas because only then could Americans compete with the giant "combines" and cartels of European business. This approach obviously did not resemble the ideal of nineteenth-century "free enterprise." It was a new approach formulated by Washington officials (especially Herbert Hoover) so that U.S. corporations could work together to obtain needed foreign markets—or exploit such vital raw material sources as Middle East oil reserves, which British and French firms threatened to monopolize.

Associationalism had another advantage: it functioned privately and outside the glare of domestic politics. The approach was worked out in corporate board rooms or in unnoticed discussions between corporate leaders and Washington officials. The business and political elites of the 1920s wanted no interference from either Congress or foreign governments; their goal was maximum freedom of action—which also explains why they wanted nothing to do with the League of Nations or other international organizations that might tie American hands. In *American Business and Foreign Policy, 1920–1933* (1971), Joan Hoff Wilson calls this search for freedom-of-maneuver "independent internationalism." Given the expanding American interests, the term is much more accurate than the "isolationist" label usually pinned on the 1920s and 1930s.

American leaders believed that the nation's welfare depended on a healthy international system. That welfare, they assumed, included not only matters of economics but the survival of individual freedom within the United States. As Hoover declared dramatically in 1921, the American system of individualism "cannot be preserved in domestic life, if it must be abandoned in our international life." Events between 1929 and 1933 proved Hoover to be a prophet. The New York money market weakened in 1929 from overspeculation and corruption, and its weakening threatened to destroy fragile European and Japanese economic systems whose lifeblood in the 1920s had been U.S. capital. As those foreign systems collapsed, the international framework fell apart; U.S. overseas markets disappeared; and the number of unemployed Americans more than doubled between 1930 and 1933 until it reached an astronomical 25 percent. "Associationalism" and "independent internationalism" had failed to produce healthy systems at home or abroad.

Franklin D. Roosevelt moved slowly after 1933 to restore the American role in world affairs. He initially gave domestic problems priority and believed he could separate them from overseas events. His approach quickly collapsed. Because of American economic and potential military power, the United States was inevitably involved in world politics. Even the so-called "isolationists" in Congress from midwestern and Rocky Mountain states had spokesmen, such as Republican Senator William Borah of Idaho, who were willing to cooperate with the Soviet Union or the new Chinese government to stop Japanese aggression. But the isolationists wanted no major involvement in European affairs or in League of Nations actions that might suck the United States into a major war. By the time of the Munich agreement between Germany, Great Britain, and France in 1938 and the outbreak of war a year later, however, the question was not whether the United States would become drawn into World War II but how.

Scholars have argued bitterly whether Roosevelt trailed, led, or simply lied to American public opinion during 1940–41. A consensus has formed that he was sensitive to and restrained by isolationist strength, but that after his third-term election victory in 1940 he secretly and steadily pushed the United States into war. Especially revealing has been the recent discovery of British Prime Minister Winston Churchill's account of his talk with FDR at the Atlantic Conference in August 1941. Speaking more than three months before the Pearl Harbor attack, Roosevelt privately declared that he so fully supported the British that he was determined to send them increased supplies—and if Hitler tried to stop the ships, it would create an "incident" that could carry the United States fully into the war.

In studying the events that led to the Japanese attack on Pearl Harbor, historians have divided over the question of whether a settlement might have been possible with Japan. Akira Iriye's *Power and Culture: the Japanese-American War, 1941–1945* (1981) argues that Washington and Tokyo officials shared common views about restructuring the world community and, specifically, the appropriate development of China. John Dower, in *War without Mercy: Race and Power in the Pacific War* (1986), has vigorously disagreed. Dower concludes that each side held views based on indigenous racial, religious, and political prejudices that led to mutual hatred, not shared assumptions. Iriye's and Dower's work on racial stereotypes in the 1940s resembles the analyses by Horsman and Hietala, who explored racism to provide insights into middle nineteenth-century diplomacy. Such examinations of internal beliefs provide major explanations of the nation's foreign policies.

More work has been published on the emergence of the Cold War in the 1940s than on any other topic in American diplomatic history. The first accounts, appearing in the 1940s and 1950s, focused on political events (such as the Yalta and Potsdam summit conferences of 1945) and blamed the Soviets for starting the Cold War. Fresh scholarship in the 1960s, however, stressed the role of economic factors and argued that the United States—which enjoyed great economic advantages as well as a monopoly on the atomic bomb in the 1940s—bore heavy responsibility for the conflict. Washington officials were especially criticized for insisting on challenging Soviet security even in the Russian border regions of eastern Europe, Iran, Greece, and Turkey. Other historians emphasized the role of individuals: the inexperienced and insecure Truman, who, some believe, reversed Roosevelt's policies aimed at cooperating with the Soviets; or the brutal Stalin, whose growing paranoia made him irrationally determined to dominate Europe and Asia.

The most influential scholarship, however, has not stressed isolated political, economic, or individual causes; it has instead insisted that the Cold War arose out of the clash of two systems. The American system valued certain individual freedoms that U.S. officials believed required an open, capitalist world. As Truman declared in a major foreign policy speech of March 6, 1947, "freedom of worship" and "freedom of speech" are "related" to "freedom of enterprise." Because of that perceived relationship, the United States opposed the Soviet system, which destroyed many economic and personal freedoms in eastern Europe. Also because of that perceived relationship, U.S. officials moved to dismantle the French and British colonial empires that had long discriminated against American freedom of enterprise in such regions as French Indochina and British protectorates in the Middle East. The United States helped force the British and French to quit their colonial areas and find security in an American-dominated alliance system.

McCormick's *American Half-Century* and Thomas Paterson's incisive book *On Every Front: The Making of the Cold War* (1979) use different approaches to view the Cold War as a competition between two historical systems rather than as a result, say, of Truman's insecurity or political mistakes made at Yalta. Deep-rooted traditions in both the United States and the Soviet Union that closely tie domestic needs to foreign policies now seem a more helpful explanation of the Cold War than do individuals or individual events in the 1940s. And the effectiveness or ineffectiveness of those traditions in pushing forward Soviet or American national interests is now seen to have depended on the evolving international arena—whose other actors in such countries as Vietnam and Afghanistan have, since the 1950s, increasingly pushed back.

Within the American tradition of foreign policy, scholars have recently paid special attention to two topics. The first is the role played by peace groups. Charles DeBenedetti's overviews trace the movement's importance back to the War of 1812. World War I, however, was again a turningpoint. During and immediately after that conflict, peace groups were directed by secular as well as religious concerns, attracted people from many sectors of the society, devised nonviolent methods for resisting war, and became a major force for cooperative, internationalist peace efforts. The antiwar movement received headlines during the post-1960 Vietnam and Central American conflicts, but it was shaped decades earlier.

A second topic that has drawn attention is the role of the changing Constitution and, especially, presidential powers in shaping foreign policy. Surprisingly, historians had devoted little attention to this fundamental relationship between constitutional rights and the execution of diplomacy until Richard Nixon blatantly abused his powers between 1970 and 1973. Abram D. Sofaer's *War, Foreign Affairs, and the Constitutional Power* (1976) demonstrates that 150 years before the "imperial presidency" of Nixon and Lyndon Johnson, the first chief executives—especially Jefferson—began to upset the system's checks and balances.

No topic in U.S. diplomatic history is more important than the changing relationship between constitutionally guaranteed freedoms at home and the exercise of American power abroad. U.S. interests, confined to thirteen seacoast colonies in 1776, had shaped global affairs by 1945. American diplomatic history, once viewed as consisting of conversations between elite officials, has become the study of how a complex domestic political economy transformed a "rising empire" into an established global empire by the late 1940s. The effects of that empire on the larger international system and, especially, on the constitutional freedoms that the foreign policy was supposed to protect are, however, only beginning to be understood.

BIBLIOGRAPHY

These sources, in addition to those identified by title in the text, are selected from recent works in U.S. diplomatic history to 1945.

Becker, William H., and Samuel F. Wells, Jr., eds. *Economics and World Power: An Assessment of American Diplomacy since 1789.* New York: Columbia University Press, 1984.

Beisner, Robert L. *From the Old Diplomacy to the New, 1865–1900.* 2d ed. Arlington Heights, Ill.: Harlan Davidson, 1986.

Cohen, Warren, ed. *New Frontiers in American–East Asian Relations.* New York: Columbia University Press, 1983.

Cole, Wayne S. *Roosevelt and the Isolationists, 1932–1945.* Lincoln: University of Nebraska Press, 1983.

Costigliola, Frank. *Awkward Dominion: American Political, Economic, and Cultural Relations with Europe, 1919–1933.* Ithaca, N.Y.: Cornell University Press, 1984.

Dallek, Robert. *Franklin D. Roosevelt and American Foreign Policy, 1932–1945.* New York: Oxford University Press, 1979.

DeBenedetti, Charles, ed. *Peace Heroes in Twentieth-Century America*. Bloomington: Indiana University Press, 1986.

Fisher, Louis. *Constitutional Conflicts between Congress and the President*. Princeton, N.J.: Princeton University Press, 1985.

Gardner, Lloyd. *Safe for Democracy: The Anglo-American Response to Revolution, 1913–1923*. New York: Oxford University Press, 1984.

Graebner, Norman. *America as a World Power: A Realist Appraisal from Wilson to Reagan*. Wilmington, Del.: Scholarly Resources, 1984.

Healy, David. *Drive to Hegemony: The United States in the Caribbean*. Madison: University of Wisconsin Press, 1988.

Kolko, Gabriel. *The Politics of War: The World and U.S. Foreign Policy, 1943–1945*. New York: Random House, 1968.

Leffler, Melvyn P. *The Elusive Quest: America's Pursuit of European Stability and French Security, 1919–1933*. Chapel Hill: University of North Carolina Press, 1979.

Link, Arthur S., ed. *Woodrow Wilson and a Revolutionary World, 1913–1921*. Chapel Hill: University of North Carolina Press, 1982.

Little, Douglas. *Malevolent Neutrality: The United States, Great Britain, and the Origins of the Spanish Civil War*. Ithaca, N.Y.: Cornell University Press, 1985.

McCormick, Thomas J. "Drift or Mastery: A Corporatist Synthesis for American Diplomatic History." *Reviews in American History* 10 (December 1982): 318–29.

Remini, Robert V. *Andrew Jackson and the Course of American Empire*. New York: Harper & Row, 1977.

Rosenberg, Emily. *Spreading the American Dream: American Economic and Cultural Expansion, 1890–1945*. New York: Hill & Wang, 1982.

Vevier, Charles. "American Continentalism: An Idea of Expansion, 1845–1910." *American Historical Review* 65 (January 1960): 323–35.